YOU AND YOUR LAWSUIT

An Insider's Guide to Saving Money

VIKTORIA MORGAN

Midnight Shadow Publishing

Published by Midnight Shadow Publishing
2505 Clearview Avenue
Ventura, CA   93001

Printed by Outskirts Press, Inc
1-888-672-6657

ISBN 10: 1-59800-828-5
ISBN 13: 978-1-59800-828-9

© Midnight Shadow Publishing, 2006
2505 Clearview Avenue, Ventura CA 93001
Phone 805.676.3464

www.MidnightShadow.net

Outskirts Press and the "OP" logo are trademarks belonging to
Outskirts Press, Inc.

Printed in the United States of America

<u>DISCLAIMER</u>

"LEGAL INFORMATION IS NOT LEGAL ADVICE"

The purpose of this book is to provide information to help readers understand the mechanics of a lawsuit. This book provides information regarding the typical procedures one might encounter and gives the reader tips on how to save money during the course of those procedures.

This book in no way constitutes legal advice.

I strongly recommend you consult with an attorney
for a legal consultation regarding your issues and case.

Table of Contents

Notes and Questions

Things I need to discuss with my attorney during this phase of the lawsuit.

Phase 1:

Issues between Parties

So, you can't seem to resolve the issues and decided you need to find a lawyer.

Initially a lawsuit begins because there is an unresolved issue between two or more parties. There are different kinds of lawsuits such as divorce, custody, child support proceedings, civil litigation, business litigation, real estate, estate planning and wills, criminal law, as well as a multitude of other types of situations. Criminal law procedures are not discussed herein. If you are looking for information about criminal law you need to find a criminal attorney.

Once you conclude you are unable to resolve your issue without the help of a lawyer, you need to choose and hire your attorney. There are advantages and disadvantages of hiring an established, well known, and sometimes expensive attorney over hiring a new, less experienced, and usually less expensive attorney. While a well-known attorney may have more experience in the field, they may likely be

TERMS YOU NEED TO KNOW

Plaintiff:	Person who initiates the lawsuit
Defendant:	Person who is defending a lawsuit.
Caption:	Section of pleading which indicates parties, court and title of the document.
Budget:	Budget of expected or projected costs associated with each phase of the suit.
Pleading:	Document created within specific guidelines, such as spacing, line numbers, with a caption, which is filed with the court.
Complaint:	Pleading filed with the court by plaintiff to initiate the lawsuit.
Answer:	Pleading filed with the court by defendant responding to the allegations contained in the Complaint.
Process Server:	Person hired to personally hand a copy of the Complaint to the defendant.
Litigation:	The filing and prosecution of your lawsuit!

Notes and Questions

very costly, when a newer more competitively priced attorney may be equally qualified to handle your case. It has been my experience that hiring a "new attorney" can be well worth the risk as many are quite competent and have that 'new' attorney drive. You may also have to consider choosing between a big firm, a small firm or sole attorney. The larger firms may have strict policies regarding fees, rates, and required retainer amounts and there may be less room for negotiation. A sole practitioner who has his or her own office will probably allow more bargaining room as far as fees, rates, required retainer amounts, etc.

One of the first things you should request once you hire your attorney is a proposed budget. The proposed budget should outline the costs associated within each phase of the lawsuit. Below is a list of line items which should be included in this proposed budget:

- Overall Case Assessment
- Fact Development Costs
- Expert's or Consultant's Costs
- Document Management Costs
- Settlement Costs, including settlement amount
- Pleading Preparation Costs
- Motion Costs, including document preparation and appearances at hearings
- Written Discovery Costs
- Document Production Costs
- Deposition Costs, including preparation, document preparation and Transcriber fees
- Expert Discovery Costs, including expert's fees and document preparation
- Witness Preparation Costs, including expert's fees and document preparation
- Trial Preparation Costs (attorney and staff preparation time)
- Pre-Trial Document Preparation Costs, including exhibit preparation and copy fees
- Trial Attendance Costs, including any staff attendance which will be billed
- Post Trial Costs, including documents preparation, hearings, and submission costs
- Expenses, including copy costs, postage, printing, fax charges, telephone or long distance charges, travel expenses, witness fees, court fees, subpoena fees, expert fees, trial exhibits, mediator's fees, and any other fees the firm is expected to pay up front on your behalf.

Your attorney should be able to project, or estimate, how much each phase will cost if the case proceeds as planned. This is a good tool that will help to keep you informed about where your money is expected to be spent. This will also help your attorney stay focused. The proposed budget is a guideline of proposed costs and should not be used as a final cost for any aspect of the case. If you are not sure what each item entails, ask your attorney to define each term. With this guideline

Notes and Questions

you can better understand how to budget your own money to cover the various costs as they become due.

When you are initiating the lawsuit, your attorney will file documents with the court which will require a specific format required by the court. In most cases, the first document filed with the court is the Complaint. The caption seen in **Figure 1.1** is an example to show you where you will find the name of the attorney, the court, the parties involved and the title of the document. Basic information can be found in the caption, in the pretty much the same spot, on most documents in most states. The documents may look slightly different, but you can usually find what you are looking for quickly in the caption area. Within the body of the Complaint, the issues of your case will be laid out specifically, separately and concisely. The final section of the Complaint contains the Prayer. The Prayer states what you would like to happen or, more specifically, what you would like the Judge to Order.

JOE ATTORNEY
LAWFIRM
123 STREET
TOWN, STATE 12345

Attorney for Plaintiff

IN THE FIRST JUDICIAL DISTRICT OF THE STATE OF __________

FOR THE COUNTY OF ___________

JANE DOE,	)	Case No.: No. 2005-1234
	)	
Plaintiff,	)	COMPLAINT
	)	
vs.	)	
	)	
JOHN DOE,	)	
	)	
Defendant	)	

FIGURE 1.1 Sample Caption format

The complaint must be personally served on the defendant. This is usually handled by your attorney's office who will hire a Process Server to find and physically hand a copy of the Complaint

TIP: You can save roughly $40 to $50 dollars if you have someone you know serve the Complaint on the defendant. Use this tip cautiously, however, since you don't want to put your friends in the middle of your suit.

Notes and Questions

and Summons to the defendant. The Process Server then completes an Affidavit of Service. A typical Affidavit of Service, which would be filed with the court, is shown below in **Figure 1.2**.

On the date the Complaint is hand delivered to the Defendant, the Defendant will have a specific number of days within which to answer the claims outlined in the Complaint. The Answer, like the Complaint, must be submitted to the court clerk and must follow the specific format required by the court. If the Defendant does not respond within the time frame specified in the Summons, the Plaintiff may file for a default and the Defendant could lose their case. This very rarely happens, so I would not count on it. Most Complaints are timely Answered. Depending on the issues and the style of the responding attorney, the Defendant may assert Affirmative Defenses or a Counterclaim against the Plaintiff within his/her Answer. In any event, at the end of the Answer, the Defendant will also have a Prayer requesting the Judge to Order things in the Defendant's favor.

JOE ATTORNEY
LAWFIRM
123 STREET
TOWN, STATE 12345

Attorney for Plaintiff

IN THE FIRST JUDICIAL DISTRICT OF THE STATE OF _______

FOR THE COUNTY OF _________

JANE DOE,   )   Case No.: No. 2005-1234
)
       Plaintiff,   )   AFFIDAVIT OF SERVICE
)
)
   vs.   )
)
)
JOHN DOE,   )
)
       Defendant
____

STATE OF _________   )
                                ss.
County of _________   )

PERSON, being first duly sworn upon oath, deposes and says:

Notes and Questions

That I am a citizen of the State of __________, over the age of eighteen (18) years, and not

a party to the above-entitled action.

That on the ______ day of <u>Month</u>, 2005, I served a true and correct copy of the following:

Summons and Complaint upon John Doe, at 123 Street address, town, City, Zip.

DATED this __________ day of February, 2007.

____

Person, Affiant

SUBSCRIBED and SWORN to before me this ______ day of February, 2007.

Notary Public for the State of _______
Residing at ____________________
Comm. Exp. ____________________

FIGURE 1.2 Sample Affidavit of Service

If you have been served legal documents, you need to see an attorney right away to preserve your legal rights and ensure you are legally protected.

At this time, some judges may require the parties to attend mediation. The whole point of mediation is to get the parties together with a third person who helps the parties settle some, if not all, of the unresolved issues. A lot of the less contentious situations can be settled, leaving only the most difficult issues to be dealt with at trial. Mediation is a far less expensive avenue to resolve issues and most cases can benefit in some way from attending mediation. The expense involved in having the Judge decide every little thing can be sky-high.

You have now entered into litigation!!!! Aren't you excited??? I didn't think so. Most people aren't.

Once you have entered into litigation, there are several things you can do to minimize your costs. Below I have listed several tips on how to do that during this first phase of the lawsuit. Not

Notes and Questions

all of these are sure-fire, however, these ideas will get you going. You will think of some of your own once you get the idea. So here we go, hang on to those pocketbooks!

Other Things and Ways to Save, Phase 1

($) Every minute of your attorney's time is money out of your pocket!

($) Pay attention….. to everything.

($) When discussing the attorney's rate, try to bargain for a flat fee, hybrid fee or a rate range. Flat fees are one fee for all work done on your case. Hybrid fees are flat fees if the attorney can get the case settled before a certain point, then a percentage, or an hourly fee, for any work after that defined point. A rate range is a range of hourly fees that may begin at $150 per hour for any work performed prior to trial and if you go to trial, any work done at trial or after is $250 per hour. Chances are you'll settle before trial and you will have saved money by paying a lower pre-trial rate. Keep in mind, however, if you go to trial you will be paying quite a hefty hourly rate. This gives you incentive to settle prior to trial!

($) Understand how the billing works. Ask if the attorney bills in quarter hour increments or six minute increments. For example: Most attorneys bill in 6 minute increments. You call, talk for 3 minutes and you are billed 0.1 hours or 6 minutes. At $200 per hour that's a $20 call. ($200x0.1=$20.00) If the attorney bills in quarter hour increments, you talk for 3 minutes and are billed 0.25 or 15 minutes which is a hefty $50 phone call. ($200x0.25=$50.00) You should also be aware of what your bill will look like and how to understand it. Is it line item, block billing, monthly, quarterly? Does it indicate who each person working on your file is and what their rate is, etc. Know exactly what to expect on your bill. With the new computer programs out today, each client could have a bill uniquely designed to their specifications.

($) Request line item billing. No block billing. Block billing is when you see several items on your bill listed together with one block of time. For example, if your bill has an entry that reads: Letter to client, Telephone call with client, draft Answer - 2.4 hours. Request the attorney list each item separately. For example, Telephone call 0.1, Letter to client 0.2, Telephone conference with opposing counsel 0.3 and so on…. You will then be able to see how much time is actually spent on what activity. The line item billing creates less opportunity for the attorney, or billing staff person, to lump a bunch of stuff together and put a long time entry on it.

($) Discuss with your attorney whether or not he/she thinks he/she can settle your matter without the necessity of going to court or even filing the suit.

($) Hire an attorney who specializes in your type of case. Ask what his/her usual kind of case load involves. Find out what the attorney's specialty is and decide if that is what you are looking for and what you need. You might not want to hire a real estate attorney to do your divorce.

Notes and Questions

(💰) Discuss fax, FedEx, runner's fees and copy charges. Are you expected to pay for incoming faxes only or outgoing, or both? Copy charges? How much per page? Do you have to pay for the FedEx when it could have been mailed U.S.P.S.? A runner fee? Are you being charged for a runner when the documents could have been mailed? Ask questions about how much you will be charged for each of these items.

(💰) Request the use of associates on standard documents and hearings. Know what the associate rate is and ask about the qualifications of the associate who will be used on your matter.

(💰) Be aware of "billable hours" vs. "overhead". Overhead is what would be considered part of the deal when you hire the attorney. For example, when the attorney drafts a letter and has his secretary put that letter into a more formal format for mailing, that secretary's time would normally be considered part of the deal, or overhead, and you would not be billed for her time. Make sure you have a clear understanding as to what will be billed, and whose time will be billed. Know if the secretary's time will be billed and at what rate. Ask what is considered "overhead" so you'll know what to expect to see on your bill and have it clearly defined so there isn't any confusion later.

(💰) If the firm utilizes paralegals, be familiar with the rate of the paralegal working on your file. Most paralegals are quite experienced and knowledgeable and much less expensive. Besides, the attorney is required to oversee all of the paralegal's work.

(💰) **READ YOUR BILLS**, all of them, every last line. Make sure all entries are related to your case. There are instances when something is erroneously miss-billed. Mistakes happen. Watch for such mistakes on your bill.

(💰) Pay your bills, on time. Be a "good" client and keep up on your bill. If the attorney – client relationship breaks down, it will cost you far more in the long run. Especially if you have to hire another attorney!

(💰) Create a friendly relationship with the secretary or paralegal. If you call the attorney with a question, the meter starts running, but you might call the secretary and possibly receive answers to your questions without being billed for the call.

(💰) When calling the office, have a list of questions written down. Plan ahead, don't call on a whim. Know what you want to know, ask it, and hang up.

(💰) You are billed for every minute you are on the phone. If you call three times in one day, you are billed on three separate entries or line items. If you talk to the paralegal or attorney for 2 minutes each time, you are billed for a total of 18 minutes for an attorney billing at six minute increments, rather than the actual 6 minutes. That's a difference of $40. This sounds like a small amount but it adds up FAST. If you can ask all your questions in one phone call you will save a bundle. Its simple math; $200x0.3=$60 whereas $200x0.1=$20.

Notes and Questions

💰 Sometimes you can negotiate or reduce your total amount due. You may not have something completely removed from your bill, but you can possibly have the balance reduced. For example, you have a very large copy job done and you are billed $450. Nobody is excited about paying $450 for copies, so call and <u>ask</u> for a reduction of this amount. You probably won't receive a total credit, but you may receive a reduced amount, say by $50 to $150. If it is reduced <u>any</u> then you are ahead of the game. It never hurts to ask, but make sure you don't make a habit of it.

💰 Watch **your** clock when speaking to a billing staff person. Keep a log of the date, time, length of call and person to whom you spoke. When the bill comes in, cross reference! Make sure you are being billed for the person with whom you spoke and at the rate which you were told you would be charged for that person. For example, if you spoke with the paralegal, who is billed at a rate of $100/hr and on the bill you were billed for the attorney's time, who bills at a rate of $200/hr, you will want to be aware of such a thing and bring it up to the attorney. (As a side note, please consider that it could be a mistake and give the staff person the courtesy of the benefit of the doubt. Now is not the time to be throwing around accusations of being "ripped off.")

💰 Always treat the staff with respect. If they like you, you will get much more done and occasionally for free! Understand you are not the only case the attorney has and things take time. Being hostile and rude is not the way to get your case finalized quickly and efficiently. It does not matter who you are or how much money you have…… be nice!

💰 When you hire the attorney, you are signing a contract for his/her services. On the contract there should be a space for "other" things…… use this space to define the things you have negotiated. Get it in writing and eliminate any confusion later on if you need to dispute an entry on your bill. Attorneys are all about getting it in writing; they shouldn't be offended and will understand your position. Remember, **If it isn't in writing, it didn't happen.**

💰 Keep a calendar of what is scheduled, things required, due dates, hearings, etc. If you see something should have happened, or should be happening, then you'll expect to see it on the bill. If it isn't happening you can call to discuss it with the secretary. Keep on top of your own case; keep it moving forward toward resolution.

💰 Faster settlement = lower fees.

💰 Discuss a term called "value billing" with your attorney. Are you going to be billed for the actual time spent on your matter? Value billing is loosely defined as follows: the stock documents took the attorney <u>xxx</u> amount of time to create the first time he/she created them. The attorney who "value bills" will bill all subsequent clients the amount of time it took to prepare the document in the first place. For example, a generic Complaint for Divorce may have taken the attorney 1.5 hours to create the first time. Any client thereafter, who would use a generic Complaint for Divorce, will have the benefit of the pleading already having been done. Will that client be billed for the actual time of putting in their specifics and caption or will that client be 'value billed' for

Notes and Questions

the amount it should have taken to write the document. It's nearly impossible to know if you are being value billed, however, you should be aware of it and discuss it with your attorney.

- 💰 Even though your matter is emotionally overwhelming, you need to READ, READ, READ the letters and documents sent to you by your attorney. If you read it and still do not understand the document, call the office, but first read the entire document or letter. Nearly everything you need to know is included in the letter or document.

- 💰 If you are expecting a settlement or money judgment, be sure to ask your attorney about any tax consequences.   Sometimes the money isn't worth it.

- 💰 Don't get "involved" with your attorney. It will only cloud his/her vision, disrupt your process, and slow matters. If you have an interest, pursue it after your matter is finalized.

- 💰 Negotiate with the attorney. Negotiate everything possible. If you don't ask for it, you won't get it.

If you already have an attorney.....

- Negotiate some of the things outlined above with your current attorney. You may not be able to receive a credit for bills already paid, however, you may be able to negotiate some discounts during the remainder of your suit. Just being more aware of things will save you money in the end.

Now that you have entered into litigation, either by filing the Complaint or Answering it, you have chosen your attorney, you have negotiated as much as you could with the attorney, you understand what to expect from your attorney and his staff, let's get into the meat of the lawsuit and what to expect during Phase 2.

Phase 2, or the Discovery Phase, is all about information. During the Discovery Phase, you will be receiving lots of information and producing lots of information. This process is both very time consuming and overwhelming. There is so much information going back and forth. The better you understand what to expect during the discovery phase, the easier it is and the more money you will likely save.

Notes and Questions

Things I need to discuss with my attorney during this phase of the lawsuit.

Phase 2:

The Discovery Phase

Time for the discovery of information.

S o you have now entered the information gathering phase which is formally called the Discovery Phase. To some, this is also known to some as the Twilight Zone. The discovery phase of the lawsuit is usually the longest. It can take months, even years, to complete. There are several different discovery tools that may be used. Not all of them are used in every matter, and quite frankly, you don't want them to be as it can become exhaustive and quite expensive.

The tools of Discovery can include Interrogatories, Request for Production of Documents and Things, Request for Admissions, Deposition, and Deposition Duces Tecum. All of the discovery tools are responded to under oath. This means you are swearing the information you provide to be true and correct to the best of your knowledge. So, keep this in mind when responding to any

TERMS YOU NEED TO KNOW	
Production of Documents:	Written requests for copies of documents and things.
Requests for Admissions:	Written requests for admissions or denials of material facts.
Deposition Duces Tecum:	Interview of a party by the other parties lawyer, requiring you bring with you specific documents listed in the Notice.
Discovery:	Information gathering phase of the lawsuit.
Interrogatories:	Written questions from one party to the other.
Deposition:	Interview of a party by the opposing attorney.
Notice:	Pleading filed with the court requesting your attendance at a deposition.
Deponent:	Person being questioned at a deposition.
Court Reporter:	Person who types every word spoken at a deposition to create a written transcript of the deposition.

Notes and Questions 

of the discovery tools used in your matter.

Let's begin with Interrogatories. This word is phonetically broken up and pronounced In'ter'rog'a-tor'y. Interrogatories are a written set of questions which each require an individual response. Most states have limits on the number of Interrogatories, or questions that can be asked. Examples of some of the kinds of questions you may see, as well as a common format for the document, are shown in **Figure 2.1**. The questions you must answer in the Interrogatories can be dreadful and make you incredibly anxious or even angry. I've included what would normally be considered "stock" Interrogatories in Figure 2.1 to give you an idea of what to expect. You may receive fewer, or more, questions, depending on your case issues and even the attorneys involved. The Interrogatory questions can ask you pretty much anything. That's one of the pitfalls of being involved in the lawsuit; however, it can also be used to your advantage. The example in Figure 2.1 is used specifically for divorce proceedings. If your matter is business related, you will most likely see a completely different set of questions. The point is to understand what the documents look like and to get the message that the discovery phase is one of gathering information, and Interrogatories are one of the tools used by the attorneys.

Interrogatories usually come in "sets". For example, Plaintiff's First Set of Interrogatories, Plaintiff's Second Set of Interrogatories, and so on. If you receive a Second Set of Interrogatories, those should be numbered sequentially where the first set left off. If the first set was numbered 1 through 22, then the second set should be numbered 23 through XX in order to keep track of the number of questions asked as well as the responses.

The following is an example stock divorce interrogatories for your review and information…. horrible, isn't it? Hang in there and keep on track, it gets easier as you go. Be sure to make notes next to the questions or interrogatories which you think may pertain to you, or which you might want to ask your attorney about. Remember these are just samples of the kinds of questions you might be asked.

Notes and Questions

JOE ATTORNEY
LAWFIRM
123 STREET
TOWN, STATE 12345
Attorney for Plaintiff

IN THE FIRST JUDICIAL DISTRICT OF THE STATE OF _______
FOR THE COUNTY OF ____________

JANE DOE,	) Case No.: No. 2005-1234
	)
Plaintiff,	) PLAINTIFF'S FIRST SET OF
vs.	) INTERROGATORIES
	)
JOHN DOE,	)
	)
Defendant	)

YOU WILL PLEASE TAKE NOTICE that JANE DOE, by and through her attorney of record, Joe Attorney, requires you to answer and respond, under each, to the following Interrogatories within ____________ days from the service hereof and in conformance with all provisions of the Rules of Civil Procedure.

In answering and responding to these discovery requests, furnish all information available to you, including information in the possession of your attorneys (and investigators, experts, etc., retained by you and your attorneys), not merely information known of your personal knowledge.

If you cannot answer or respond to the following in full, after exercising due diligence to secure the information or documents to do so, please so state, and respond to the extent possible, specifying your inability to respond to the remainder, and stating whatever information and knowledge you have concerning the portion not responded to.

These discovery requests are deemed continuing requests, and your responses thereto are to be supplemented as additional information and knowledge becomes available or known to you.

If you contend that any discovery request seeks the disclosure of matters protected by the

Notes and Questions

attorney/client privilege or work product doctrine, please identify (as defined below) the matters you allege are protected against disclosure.

DEFINITIONS

The following definitions apply whenever the defined word appears in the following Interrogatories and Requests for Production, except as otherwise expressly indicated:

(a) The words "you" or "your" refer to the above named responding party, and all of his/her agents, representatives, and employees. Where knowledge, information, or documents in your custody, control, or possession is requested or referred to, such request includes all relevant knowledge, information, or documents in the custody, control, or possession of you and all of your agents, representatives, and employees.

(b) The word "person" means any individual, partnership, corporation, trade association, government agency, or instrumentality, or any other entity, or any director, officer, employee, or agent thereof.

(c) The word "document" or "documents" means the original, all non identical copies, and all drafts of writings or visual representations of information of any kind. This includes, but is not limited to, correspondence, memoranda, reports, minutes, pamphlets, photographs or the like, pictures, films, notes, letters, telegrams, invoices, orders, forecasts, appraisals, messages (including reports, notes, logs and memoranda or concerning telephone conversations and conferences), calendar and diary entries, summaries, schedules, records, computerized data, computer programs, graphics, sketches, telegrams, telexes, transcripts, graphs, charts and compilations. It also includes videotape or sound recordings, and any similar method of recording information. All attachments or enclosures to a document are deemed to be part of such document.

Notes and Questions

(d) The word "identify" with respect to a person means to provide the name, title and last known home address and telephone number of such person, as well as the name, address, and telephone number of the last known place of business where such person is or was employed, assigned, or headquartered.

(e) The word "identify" with respect to documents, reports, or exhibits means to state the author or creator, addressee(s), persons copied, date, subject matter, title if any, and the nature of the document (e.g., letter, memorandum, chart, etc.), and shall refer to all documents, reports or exhibits within the possession, custody or control of the above named responding party, or any of his agents, representatives and attorneys. If you are not in possession, custody, or control of any such document but know or understand that such a document exists, "identify" shall mean to provide the information outlined above in this definitional paragraph and shall also mean to identify the person that does possess or have custody or control of the document, with sufficient specificity to permit the document to be requested by subpoena.

(f) The word "identify" with respect to occurrences, incidents, or events means to state with specificity the location, date, and time of the occurrence or event, and to describe completely and in detail what transpired.

(g) The word "knowledge" includes first hand knowledge and information derived from any other source including, but not limited to, knowledge based on hearsay.

INTERROGATORIES

INTERROGATORY NO. 1: PERSONS ANSWERING. Please state the name, address and telephone number of each person answering these Interrogatories.

INTERROGATORY NO. 2: ASSETS. List separately under each of the following categories

Notes and Questions

each and every asset that you own, in which you have an interest, or in which you claim an interest, and include assets held for you by another person or entity. Next to each asset state the fair market value of the asset. State next to each asset the basis of how you determined the fair market value of an asset, e.g. bank statement, my personal opinion, tax assessment, etc.

Category A: All bank accounts, savings accounts, credit union accounts, and brokerage house accounts. As to each account, include the name and location of the institution, the account number, and identify each person having signature authority on the account.

Category B: All funds held by you or for your benefit which are not contained within an account, including cash on hand or held for you by another.

Category C: All securities, including but not limited to stock, stock options, bonds and mutual funds accounts. As to each option and account, include the name and location of the institution, the account number, and the identity of each person having a signature authority on the account.

Category D: All business interests, including but not limited to, sole proprietorships, corporations, partnerships, limited partnerships, and other entities in which you have an interest. As to each, describe the entity , identify all other persons or entities having an interest therein, describe the extent of your interest, state when your interest was acquired, identify the source of the funds used to acquire the interest, and separately state the value of the entity as a whole, as well as the value of your interest therein.

Category E: All pension plans, profit sharing plans, individual retirement accounts and any other retirement plans.

Category F: All life insurance policies held by you or on your life and the cash value thereof, including as to each policy the insurance company name, policy number and current named

Notes and Questions

beneficiaries.

Category G: All real estate rights, including address and legal description, and as to each property indicate the date of purchase, the purchase price, the source of the funds for purchase, describe any encumbrances thereon, and identify the current owners of record.

Category H: All personal property including vehicles, boats, vessels, recreational vehicles, furnishings, appliances, household goods, equipment, electronics, etc.

Category I: All benefits of your employment, including future rights to receive income, mileage, bonuses, vacation time, sick time, and deferred earnings. Describe specifically the reasons for the deferral and the terms upon which payment will be made.

Category J: All safety deposit boxes, portable safes, storage units or other secured receptacles owned by you, held for your benefit, or that you are holding for the benefit of another. As to each, include the location, account or reference number, contents, and identify each person, their address and telephone number, who has access or authority to access.

Category K: All other assets.

<u>INTERROGATORY NO. 3:</u> SALE OF PROPERTY. If you have sold any property during the past twenty-four (24) months, list the item sold, date of sale, the amount received for each item and the name of the person or entity that purchased the property from you.

<u>INTERROGATORY NO. 4:</u> SEPARATE PROPERTY. If you claim any of the property listed in your answers as your separate property:

A. State the property you contend to be your separate property;

B. State all the facts upon which you are relying to support your contention that the property is your separate property;

Notes and Questions

C. Describe in detail each document which you believe supports your contention that the property is your separate property;

D. State the present fair market value of the item you claim to be your separate property.

INTERROGATORY NO. 5: REPAID LOAN. What loans have you repaid in the last six (6) months?

INTERROGATORY NO. 6: FINANCIAL STATEMENTS. Have you given any financial statements in the two (2) years preceding this date? If so, specify the person or entity to which you supplied a financial statement and if you will do so without a Motion for Production, attach copies of any such financial statements to your Answers to these Interrogatories.

INTERROGATORY NO. 7: INCOME. State your total gross income and your total net income for the two (2) full years immediately preceding this date and the amount of your gross monthly income and our net monthly income for the month immediately preceding the date of these Interrogatories.

INTERROGATORY NO. 8: DEBTS. List all debts that you now owe indicating the name, address and telephone number of each person to whom you owe money, specifying the amount of money owed to each person or entity, explaining what each debt was incurred for and identifying all debts that you contend are community debts.

INTERROGATORY NO. 9: MONTHLY LIVING EXPENSES. Itemize your current monthly living expenses and specify the amount paid each month on any of the debts referred to herein.

INTERROGATORY NO. 10: PROPERTY TO BE AWARDED TO THE PLAINTIFF. List all of the property that you think the court should award to the plaintiff in this action.

Notes and Questions

INTERROGATORY NO. 11: PROPERTY TO BE AWARDED TO DEFENDANT. List

all of the property that you think the court should award to the defendant in this action.

INTERROGATORY NO. 12: DEBTS INCURRED SINCE SEPARATION. Itemize any

debts or expenses you have incurred from the date of the separation from your spouse to the

present date.

INTERROGATORY NO. 13: WITNESSES. State the name, address and telephone number

of each person you intend to call as a witness at the trial of this matter. With regard to each

witness, state the substance of the facts to which you expect the witness to testify.

INTERROGATORY NO. 14: EXPERT WITNESSES. Separately identify each person whom

you may call as an expert witness at the trial of this action and state the subject matter on which

such expert witness is expected to testify, the substance of the facts to which such expert witness

is expected to testify, and the substance of the opinions to which such expert is expected to

testify.

INTERROGATORY NO. 15: DOCUMENTARY EVIDENCE. Do you intend to introduce

any documentary evidence at the trial of this matter? If so, describe each document or exhibit you

intend to introduce.

INTERROGATORY NO. 16: ATTEMPTS TO OBTAIN EMPLOYMENT. Describe in

detail all efforts you have made in the last six (6) months to obtain employment. State the name,

address and telephone number of each person or entity you have contacted about employment

and state the name, address and telephone number of each individual or entity with whom you

have filed a formal application for employment.

INTERROGATORY NO. 17: GIFTS/LOANS. Have you loaned or given money or gifts

Notes and Questions 

with a value in excess of $25 to any relative, friend, or anyone else during your marriage to your

spouse? If so, for each person receiving such loan or gift state:

A. The name and address of the person;

B. The total amount loaned or gifted;

C. The date of each loan or gift;

D. The reason for each loan or gift;

E. A description of any consideration or evidence of indebtedness received in exchange for such

loan or gift.

F. The amount paid back or received back on such loan or gift.

DATED this _______ day of ________________, 2005.

____
JOE ATTORNEY

FIGURE 2.1 – Sample Interrogatories for typical divorce

The document should define what exactly each term means and how many days you have to respond to the questions. For Example, in some states you are allowed only fifteen (15) days to respond to the Discovery requests. That does not mean you have 15 days to respond to your attorney. That means your attorney needs to have your responses returned to the other lawyer in 15 days. You should provide the information to your attorney as quickly as possible so your attorney may respond in a timely manner. The longer you wait, the more letters and phone calls your attorney has to deal with, which in turn costs you more money!

> **TIP:** Send your responses to Interrogatory requests by email to your attorney's office. This speeds up the document preparation time. If the staff can "block and paste" your answers into the document, it will cut their preparation time down dramatically. Depending on the length of the document, this can save you hundreds of dollars by the time you are finished. Be very clear as to which request you are answering to make it as easy as possible.
> Example: **Response to Request No. 1:** Jane Doe, 555-12-1414, 444 Front Street, Village, State.

Notes and Questions 

Most commonly, you will receive Interrogatories and Request for Production of Documents at the same time, either within one document or separately. These documents frequently refer to each other in their questioning. Sometimes you can receive Interrogatories mixed with Requests for Production of Documents as well as Requests for Admissions. Each has its purpose which you will understand better once you have finished this section.

Requests for Production of Documents and Things are requests for exactly that; documents and things. These requests ask you to produce copies of documents the other side believes are important. For example, copies of bank statements, financial statements, letters, cards, kid's school report cards, savings statements, credit card statements, stock holding statements, etc.. **Figure 2.2** illustrates some requests you may see and a common format for the Requests for Documents and Things.

JOE ATTORNEY
LAWFIRM
123 STREET
TOWN, STATE 12345

Attorney for Plaintiff

IN THE FIRST JUDICIAL DISTRICT OF THE STATE OF _______
FOR THE COUNTY OF ____________

JANE DOE,	) Case No.: No. 2005-1234
	)
Plaintiff,	) **REQUEST FOR PRODUCTION OF**
	) **DOCUMENTS**
	)
vs.	)
	)
	)
JOHN DOE,	)
	)
Defendant	)

Pursuant to Rule 34 of the Rules of Civil Procedure, you are requested to produce and make

available for inspection and/or copying within _________ days from the service hereof, at

Notes and Questions

the offices of Joe Attorney at LAWFIRM, 123 Street, Town, State, 12345, the documents herein

specified.

REQUEST FOR PRODUCTION NO. 1: <u>FINANCIAL STATEMENTS</u>. The original,

or if the original is not available then a copy, of each financial statement or document of any

kind prepared by you or any other party listing your assets and/or liabilities.

REQUEST FOR PRODUCTION NO. 2: <u>RECORDS OF INCOME</u>. The original, or if

the original is not available then a copy, of each document showing your income for the

period January 1, 2000, to the present date.

REQUEST FOR PRODUCTION NO. 3: <u>INCOME TAX RETURNS</u>. Complete copies of

each state and federal income tax return filed by you at any time during the marriage.

REQUEST FOR PRODUCTION NO. 4: <u>DOCUMENTS PERTAINING TO

PROPERTY</u>. The original, or if the original is not available then copies, of any documents or

records you have describing any interest you have in any real or personal property as of the

present date.

REQUEST FOR PRODUCTION NO. 5: <u>CHECKING ACCOUNTS</u>. The original, or if

the original is not available then a copy, of each checking account document, including ledgers,

account statements, canceled checks, withdrawal slips, deposit slips, check stubs, check registers,

copies of checks and any other records pertaining to your checking accounts for each checking

account on which you were or are authorized to deposit or withdraw funds alone or with any

other party between the dates January 1, 2000, and the present date.

REQUEST FOR PRODUCTION NO. 6: <u>SAVINGS ACCOUNT RECORDS</u>. The

original, or if the original is not available then a copy, of each document pertaining to any savings

Notes and Questions 

account maintained by you between the dates January 1, 2000, and the present date.

REQUEST FOR PRODUCTION NO. 7: <u>RECORDS OF OTHER ACCOUNTS</u>. The original, or if the original is not available then a copy, of all documents pertaining to any account in which money is deposited or has been deposited from January 1, 2000, to the present date.

REQUEST FOR PRODUCTION NO. 8: <u>CREDIT CARDS</u>. The original, or if the original is not available then a copy, or each document or record reflecting any charges made by you on any credit card for the period January 1, 2000, to the present date.

REQUEST FOR PRODUCTION NO. 9: <u>EXPENSE ACCOUNT</u>. The original, or if the original is not available then a copy, of each document showing all items of expenses incurred by you in any business-related expense which was or may be reimbursed by an employer to the extent those expenses were incurred between January 1, 2000, and the present date.

REQUEST FOR PRODUCTION NO. 10: <u>RETIREMENT PLANS</u>. Copies of all documents relating to each retirement plan in which you presently have or at any time during the marriage have had any interest. This includes a copy of the summary plan description and the plan document itself.

REQUEST FOR PRODUCTION NO. 11: <u>SEPARATE PROPERTY</u>. Copies of any documents or records that you believe support your contention that any property presently owned by you is your separate property.

REQUEST FOR PRODUCTION NO. 12: <u>LIFE INSURANCE</u>. Copies of any policies of life insurance on your life that are presently in effect or that have been in effect at any time since January 1, 2000.

REQUEST FOR PRODUCTION NO. 13: <u>TRIAL EXHIBITS</u>. Copies of any documents

Notes and Questions 

that you intend to introduce into evidence at the trial of this matter.

REQUEST FOR PRODUCTION NO. 14: PURCHASES MADE IN LAST SIX (6)

MONTHS. Copies of any documentation regarding any purchases made within the last six (6)

months.

Dated this _____ day of _____________, 2005.

By: ____________________________
JOE ATTORNEY

FIGURE 2.2 Sample Requests for Production of Documents

Whether or not you agree with the request, you should provide all of the items requested to your attorney and discuss with your attorney whether or not the information <u>must</u> be produced. You and your attorney will decide if the requests are relevant or requests for what is called 'privileged' information. Privileged documents are usually documents which do not fall within the scope of the request and which are protected for a variety of reasons. For Example, all letters to and from your attorney are privileged documents. Should you and your attorney decide the information is in fact privileged, your attorney will take the necessary and proper measures to protect said information. You, on the other hand, need to provide the requested information to your attorney as quickly as possible. Sometimes it's faster, easier and cheaper to produce the documents rather than go into court to fight over whether or not you have to produce them. Only your attorney can help you decide if the information should be protected.

> **TIP:** When you receive a request, respond to it as quickly as possible. If you delay past the deadline, your attorney may receive a hearing notice and request for the judge to Order you to respond. Chances are you will have to respond anyway and you will pay several hundred dollars for the attorney to attend a hearing. If you do not want to produce something you should immediately discuss this with your attorney.

Another discovery tool is the Request for Admission. Requests For Admissions are like Interrogatories in that they are a series of written questions which must be individually answered. The format for responding to the Admission is either an admission or denial of the information stated in the request. Unlike Interrogatories, these questions have a very different result. The

Notes and Questions

responses to the requests must be received within a specific timeframe or they will be deemed admitted, which can have an adverse effect on your case. It is essential you respond to your attorney immediately whenever you see **Requests for Admissions**. Admissions are used to declare a positive affirmation or denial of a material fact or allegation at issue.

Ok, so you have responded to written questions, provided documents and admitted or denied things........what's next?

Another very common discovery tool is the Deposition. A deposition is a live interview with you, your attorney, the other person's attorney, occasionally the other party and a court reporter. The court reporter is a "typist" who takes down every word spoken on his/her special machine. Remember, Depositions are taken under oath. There are a lot of people in the room and one person, the other lawyer, asks you a whole bunch of questions. The court reporter will create a written transcript of the meeting.   It is important to be very clear in your responses to the questions asked. If you do not understand the question, say so. You can always ask the attorney to re-phrase or repeat the question. You are verifying, under oath, that your answers are true and correct so you need to know what it is you are answering. Under no circumstances should you be less than truthful. Your attorney can deal with pretty much any issue, except if you are caught in a lie under oath, not to mention other legal ramifications.

A commonly used format for a deposition notice is shown below in **Figure 2.4**. As you can see, the notice will clearly indicate the date, time, and place where you are to appear. When setting the date for your deposition, the other side may ask for your availability prior to doing so, though this is not always the case.

Notes and Questions

JOE ATTORNEY
LAWFIRM
123 STREET
TOWN, STATE 12345
Attorney for Plaintiff

IN THE FIRST JUDICIAL DISTRICT OF THE STATE OF _________
FOR THE COUNTY OF __________

JANE DOE,	) Case No.: No. 2005-1234
	)
Plaintiff,	) **NOTICE OF TAKING**
	) **DEPOSITION OF JOHN DOE**
	)
vs.	)
	) **DATE:** July 12, 2005
JOHN DOE,	) **TIME:** 10:30 a.m.
	) **PLACE:** 123 Street
Defendant	) **Town, State**

TO: THE ABOVE-NAMED Defendant, JOHN DOE and your attorney.

PLEASE TAKE NOTICE that the above-named Plaintiff will take the testimony, on oral examination before a Court Reporter or some other officer authorized to administer oaths, of JOHN DOE, at the time and place herein set forth.

> **DATE: July 12, 2005**
> **TIME: 10:30 a.m.**
> **PLACE: 123 Street, Town, State**

You are hereby notified to appear at the time and place indicated and to take part in such proceedings as you may deem proper. Oral examination will continue from day to day until completed, Sunday and holidays excepted, and you are invited to appear and take such part in the examination of the witness as is advisable and proper.

Dated this ____ day of ______________, 2005

By:_________________________________

JOE ATTORNEY

FIGURE 2.4 Sample Notice of Deposition

Notes and Questions 

At your deposition, the other side isn't just asking you questions to gather information. You are also being evaluated on how you handle yourself under pressure; how you appear as a witness, and how you will appear to the jury and/or judge. Therefore, you should be clean cut, well-rested, dressed appropriately and properly nourished (i.e. not hungry). Be very well versed on your subject matter, and clearly understand your issues and information.   The longer the deposition, the more it will cost you in the end.

Another form of deposition is the Deposition Duces Tecum. A Deposition Duces Tecum is the same as a deposition, except it also outlines specific documents and things that you must bring with you to the deposition. For example, copies of your check register, checking account statements, financial documents, etc. You are required to bring those specific documents requested

with you, the other attorney will ask questions about those documents and then those documents will become exhibits to your deposition transcript.

Sometimes a videographer will also attend the deposition. The videographer runs the video camera but does not participate in any other way. Similar to how the court reporter takes down a transcript of the words spoken, the videographer videotapes the deponent (the person being deposed) during the entirety of the deposition. Even when the deposition is being videotaped, the court reporter takes down the written transcript of every word spoken.

After you are done with your deposition, you will likely hear the attorney who asked the questions indicate to the court reporter whether or not he would like to purchase the transcript. Deposition transcripts are not a given. After the deposition your attorney decides if the transcript is needed and will then order it. Depending on the length of the deposition, it could be quite costly.

TIP: Discuss with your attorney whether or not the transcript of the deposition is needed. If not, you can save yourself a few hundred dollars by not ordering it.   If you need the transcript, it can still be ordered prior to trial.

If the transcript is ordered, you can easily add another couple of hundred dollars to your bill.

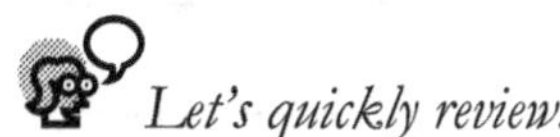

Let's quickly review.

You have entered the Discovery, or information gathering phase of the lawsuit. Within the discovery phase, you may encounter Interrogatories, Requests for Production of Documents and

Notes and Questions

Things, Request for Admissions, Depositions or Depositions Duces Tecum. Provided your attorney feels he has received all of the information necessary to move forward, you will next enter the trial preparation and trial phase of your suit.

During the Discovery phase, the longest phase, of the lawsuit, there are several ways to save money. This is probably the most important phase because of its length and the amount of your involvement. You have experienced several tools; Interrogatories, Requests for Documents, Admissions and Depositions, wherein you receive or provide information. Each tool allows you an opportunity to save money. So, here we go with those money saving tips…..

Other Things and Ways to Save, Phase 2

- (\$) Now more than ever you need to sharpen your time saving skills. Remember, every minute of your attorney's time is money out of your pocket! .

- (\$) What you can do yourself, you don't have to pay the paralegal or staff person to do for you. For example, if you can follow up on obtaining the statements from the bank as requested, you don't have to pay the paralegal or attorney to follow up with the bank for you.

- (\$) Read every document that comes to you. Most documents will have all the information you need. Prior to making a phone call to the attorney's office, read the documents in hand….You may be holding the answer to your questions in your hands.

- (\$) Be organized. The more organized you are, the easier it is for your attorney. If you have all of your documents and information in one place and organized neatly, it will be much easier for you to provide things to your attorney. If you provide your documents and information to your attorney in an organized manner, it will be easier for your attorney to put the same into formal documents. When it is easier for your attorney, it takes less of his or her time, which costs you less money.

- (\$) Respond to any and all requests as quickly as possible. If you cannot respond right away, let your attorney know. A simple letter from your attorney to the other side regarding your timeframe may save your attorney from having to prepare several court documents, attend hearings and save you several hundreds of dollars!

- (\$) Be thorough. Don't skip any questions. If you don't know the answer or don't have the answer, indicate so in your responses. Otherwise, you'll be getting a phone call. Remember….. Phone call = \$\$

Notes and Questions

- Know what kind of technology your attorney uses and take advantage of that technology. Send your responses to your attorney via email or on a disk if you have access to a computer. This saves staff members' time in preparing the documents.

- Know what kind of computer programs your attorney uses and/or is proficient in…. If you send a spreadsheet to an attorney who doesn't have the foggiest idea how to use one, you are wasting valuable dollars on him staring at the screen blankly wondering what the heck all those numbers mean. (This rarely happens nowadays, but why chance it?) If you send everything in Word and it's a WordPerfect office, there may be a problem. Most offices, however, are capable of handling both, but you should ask just to be sure.

- If you do not have access to a computer, clearly print your answers on a clean sheet of paper. Clearly mark your responses. For example,
    <u>Req. No. 1:</u> Jane Doe, 555-12-1414, 444 Front Street, Village, State.
    <u>Req. No. 2:</u> ………….. And so on….

- Discuss with your attorney, or paralegal working on your matter, what kinds of things they think you could do to help make things go smoother, easier and quicker. Communicate regularly, yet concisely, with your attorney and his/her staff.

- If you have your entire checking account on an accounting program on your home or business computer, let your attorney know. If they need to have your financial information, this may save several hours of data entry time and several hundreds of dollars. I have once heard of a client paying around $10,000 for a paralegal to enter checks into a computer accounting program when the client had it on his computer all along. A little communication could have saved him *thousands* of dollars!

- Label your discovery responses clearly. If you have a stack of documents that are all mismatched and meshed together, you'll be paying for the attorney or staff person to organize them for you. If you provide them to your attorney organized, sorted and labeled as to which requests they are responding to, you will save several hours and hundreds of dollars in preparation time.

- Read the document requests, respond by the date required, and respond to only what is requested. This is not the time to add in a bunch of documents or information that has not been asked of you. This just adds to the stack of documents to be reviewed by your attorney and it may spur the other side to ask *more* questions or request *more* documents.

- When producing documents as requested in a set of Requests for Production of Documents and Things, provide clear, full copies of your documents, single-sided and not stapled. This will allow your attorney to make copies quickly. If you are sure you have responded accurately, you can provide 2 copies to your attorney, cutting down on in-house copy fees.

Notes and Questions

$ Keep a log of any and all communications you have with your attorney's office.

$ Paralegals are qualified to perform most of the discovery legwork and should be doing so. If your firm does not utilize paralegals, request an associate attorney do the work. Both the paralegal and associate attorney are overviewed by a managing attorney or partner. Request the paralegal or associate work on the "stock discovery" documents and save your attorney/partner time and money for more complex issues.

$ Request an associate attorney attend the more basic discovery related hearings. Associate rates are far less than partner rates and associates should be able to handle these basic hearings easily.

$ Get to know the paralegal on your case and do your best to maintain a friendly cooperative relationship. Paralegals can be your best friend or your worst nightmare. Besides, once you get to know them a bit, you will have much more confidence with their competence. If you are confident in them, they will feel it and you will get a better return on your money.

$ You will be working closely with the paralegal, associate attorney or secretary. Now is an excellent time to manage that friendly relationship. Nobody admits it, but the pain in the rear client does not always get the best, most cost effective service.

$ Do not ask the paralegal for legal advice. Feel free, however, to ask the paralegal to relay questions and/or information to the attorney. This will save you the partner's billing rate while the same information is transferred.

$ Again, keep a list of questions you have and ask them at one time. Then write the answers down so you don't ask the same questions over and over…. Paying two, three or four times for the same information isn't very economical.

$ Request your attorney and staff members communicate with you via email. It's faster, cheaper and you can respond via email as well. Lots of times email communication is so quick the office forgets to bill for it.

$ Ask your attorney if they utilize scanning technology in his/her office. If so, ask all your documents to be scanned and emailed to you. This can save on postage and copy charges; and some "letter to client" charges as well. And once again, you will receive the information quickly. Be sure to discuss if you will be charged for the scanning. It's best to know exactly what you will be charged for each service <u>prior</u> to being billed.

$ When you are being deposed, be very familiar with the details of your case. This may reduce the length of the deposition, thereby saving on your attorney's hourly fees. Also, the shorter the deposition, the cheaper the cost of the court reporter's transcript.

Notes and Questions 

$ Ask your attorney to order an electronic copy of the deposition transcript if he/she decides to order the transcript at all. Electronic copies can then be e-mailed to you, or a disc provided, and you can quickly do word searches to find pertinent information. There are programs that can take 2 or 3 transcripts and simultaneously do a word search. You can then see who knows what about what very quickly. An electronic transcript can also be printed, four little transcript pages per sheet, thereby reducing your postage and copy charges.

$ Discuss with your attorney whether or not a deposition transcript is needed at this stage of the suit. If not, don't order it. You may settle the matter prior to trial and not need it at all. If you don't settle, you can always order it later. Timing is important here. Don't order it too late, or you will have to pay a rush fee.

$ Keep most of your communication focused on what you've hired your attorney to do for you. While it is an extremely difficult time in your life, keep the emotional discussions for friends and counselors and the business with the attorney. A counselor may be a much better investment for your emotional needs.

$ Every time you call your attorney's office, put a $20 dollar bill into a jar by the phone. If you speak for more than 10 minutes, you better make it two! And if you speak to the attorney, you better throw in a $50. You will need it when you receive the bill. As you look at the jar, you will quickly see how much each phone call costs. This visual aid will help you save time and money.

$ Keep your own calendar of what is due and when. Provide your responses as soon as possible and understand the timeframe involved with each deadline.

So, you are now in full swing litigation. You have gone through the initial filings, emerged from the Twilight Zone of the Discovery Phase and learned a lot about your case, their case, your attorney, and their attorney. You should now be discussing with your attorney whether or not you want to proceed to trial. If you are going to proceed, you will enter the trial preparation and trial phase of the suit. Things will move much faster now, sometimes too fast, and lots will need to be done in order to be ready for the upcoming trial.

Are you ready for the trial phase? Let's go!

Notes and Questions

Things I need to discuss with my attorney during this phase of the lawsuit.

Phase 3:

Trial Preparation and Trial

Your day in court is finally coming.

Let's review. You had an issue, could not resolve it, a suit was filed and answered and the judicial fight began. The lawsuit continued and you went through several of the discovery tools such as Interrogatories, Requests for Productions of Documents and Things, Request for Admissions and Depositions. With all of the information you have received thus far, you still feel the matter cannot be resolved and you should proceed to trial.

In the beginning so much happened, fairly quickly, then the discovery phase hit and things seemed to slow to a crawl. It's the hurry up and wait syndrome. You had to gather several documents to produce, and you received copies of several documents from the other side. Next you enter trial preparation and the trial

TERMS YOU NEED TO KNOW	
Pretrial Schedule:	Schedule set by court or Judge indicating when the required steps must be completed prior to the trial date
Pretrial Hearing:	Hearing with Judge, attorneys and parties to discuss whether the case is ready to proceed to trial.
Status Conference:	Hearing with Judge, attorneys and parties to discuss the status of the case and available dates to set trial.
Exhibits:	Documents used at trial to support your issues.
Stipulation:	Agreement between the parties.

Notes and Questions 

phase. Things seem to heat up all over again. Now, things are moving <u>very</u> quickly. In the two to four weeks prior to trial, things may seem crazy and downright unmanageable.

I love the last weeks prior to trial, it is so incredibly intense!

You and your attorney now begin serious trial preparation. From its inception, a lawsuit is preparation for trial. Most of the fine tuning exhibit preparation, however, occurs within the month prior to the trial date. When you get your trial date, or Notice of Trial, you may also receive a Pre-Trial Scheduling Order. **Figure 3.1** is an example of a Pretrial Scheduling Order. This Order outlines the pretrial deadlines which you must meet. This ensures the Judge that the case is ready for trial when your trial date finally arrives.

IN THE DISTRICT COURT OF THE FIRST JUDICIAL DISTRICT OF THE

STATE OF __________, IN AND FOR THE COUNTY OF ____________

JANE DOE,)	
)	Case No. CV ______
Plaintiff,)	
)	**SCHEDULING ORDER,**
vs.)	**NOTICE OF TRIAL SETTING**
)	**AND INITIAL PRETRIAL**
JOHN DOE,)	**ORDER**
)	
Defendant.)	
_____________________)	

Pursuant to {state code}, IT IS HEREBY ORDERED that:

1. A **JURY** trial for 3 days(s) will commence at the __________ County Courthouse at 9:00 a.m. on **06/20/2005. If possible, cases set for the same day will be tried on a to follow basis.**

2. Prior to the trial date, the Court will issue an order establishing the priority setting for each of the civil matters set for trial on the above trial date. The Court, at its discretion, may at any

Notes and Questions

time amend its order setting the priority of the cases set for trial.

Notice is hereby given that all civil trial settings are subject to being preempted by the court's criminal calendar.

In order to assist with the pretrial conference and trial of this matter **IT IS HEREBY FURTHER ORDERED** that:

1. **PRETRIAL MOTIONS:** Motions for summary judgment shall be timely filed so as to be heard **not later than ninety (90) days before trial**. The last day for filing all other pretrial motions shall be **twenty-one (21) days before trial**, except for *motions in limine* concerning witnesses and exhibits designated pursuant to paragraph nos. 6 and 7 respectively of this Pretrial Order. Motions *in limine* concerning designated witnesses and exhibits shall be submitted in writing **at least seven (7) days before trial**. Motions *in limine* concerning any designated exhibit shall attach copies of the exhibit in issue. Motions *in limine* regarding designated witnesses shall attach copies of the discovery requests claimed to require the earlier disclosure, and a representation by counsel regarding the absence of a prior response from the party to whom the discovery was directed. The fact that a party, which has submitted discovery to another party, has not filed motions to compel in advance of trial does not, in and of itself, waive an objections by that party as to the timeliness of disclosure of witnesses and exhibits by the other party as required by this order.

2. **MOTIONS FOR SUMMARY JUDGMENT:** There shall be served and filed with each motion for summary judgment a separate concise statement, together with a reference to the record, of each of the material facts as to which the moving party contends there are no genuine issues of dispute. Any party opposing the motion shall, **not later than fourteen (14) days prior to the date of the hearing**, serve and file a separate concise statement, together with a

Notes and Questions

reference to the record, setting forth all material facts as to which it is contended there exist genuine issues necessary to be litigated. In determining any motion for summary judgment, the Court may assume that the facts as claimed by the moving party are admitted to exist without controversy, except and to the extent that such facts are asserted to be actually in good faith controverted by a statement filed in opposition to the motion.

3. **BRIEFS AND MEMORANDA:** In addition to any original brief or memorandum filed with the Clerk of the Court, a chambers' copy shall be provided to the Court. To the extent counsel rely on legal authorities not contained in the _______**(state)**_____ **Reports**, a copy of each case or authority cited shall be attached to the Court's copy of the brief or memorandum.

4. **DISCOVERY DISPUTES:** Unless otherwise ordered, the Court will not entertain any discovery motion, except those brought pursuant to *civil procedure* by a person who is not a party, unless counsel for the moving party files with the Court, at the time of filing the motion, a statement showing that the lawyer making the motion has made a reasonable effort to reach agreement with opposing counsel on the matters set forth in the motion. The motion shall not refer the Court to other documents in the file. For example, if the sufficiency of an answer to an interrogatory is in issue, the motion shall contain, verbatim, both the interrogatory and the allegedly insufficient answer, followed by each party's contentions, separately stated. In the absence of a showing of good cause as to why the discovery was not initiated so that timely responses were due **at least thirty (30) days before trial**, the Court will not hear motions to compel discovery **after twenty-one (21) days before trial.**

5. **EXPERT WITNESSES:** Not later than **one hundred eighty (180) days**

Notes and Questions

before trial, plaintiff(s) shall disclose all experts to be called at trial. Not later than **one hundred fifty (150) days before trial**, defendant(s) shall disclose all experts to be called at trial. Such disclosure shall consist of at least the subject matter upon which the expert is expected to testify and the substance of any opinions to which the expert is expected to testify. The disclosure shall be contemporaneously filed with the Court.

Each party shall, **at least twenty-eight (28) days before** trial, file with the Court and serve all parties with a supplemental disclosure for each expert witness who shall identify the underlying facts and data upon which the opinions of each expert are based, to the extent such information is required to be disclosed pursuant to ***civil procedure.*** Absent good cause, an expert may not testify to matters not included in the disclosure. A party may comply with the disclosure by referencing expert witness depositions, without restating the deposition testimony in the disclosure report.

6. **REQUEST FOR PRIORITY SETTING: Sixty (60) days prior to the trial date,** counsel will advise the Court by letter to the Judge at chambers, and serve all counsel and pro se parties with a copy of the letter, as to whether counsel is requesting a priority setting; the status of settlement negotiations, and whether any demands or offers have been exchanged (without disclosing the specifics of any settlement offers or demands); whether any mediation has occurred or is scheduled; and, any other matters counsel believes pertinent to a priority setting, such as any need for advance notice for travel arrangements of witnesses or for expert witnesses. The participation of a party in mediation will be considered as a reason for granting a party's request for a priority setting.

7. **DISCLOSURE OF WITNESSES:** Each party shall prepare and exchange between the parties and filed with the Clerk **at least fourteen (14) days before trial** a list of

Notes and Questions

witnesses, with current addresses and telephone numbers, setting forth a brief statement identifying the general subject matter about which the witness may be asked to testify (exclusive of impeachment witnesses). Each party shall provide opposing parties with a list of the party's witnesses and shall provide the Court with two copies of each list of witnesses.

8.   **EXHIBIT AND EXHIBIT LISTS:** Using the attached form, each party shall prepare a list of exhibits it expects to offer. Exhibits should be listed in the order that the party anticipates they will be offered. Exhibit labels can be obtained from the court clerk. Each party shall affix labels to their exhibits before trial. After the labels are marked and attached to the original exhibit, copies should be made. Plaintiff's exhibits should be marked in numerical sequence. Defendant's exhibits should be marked in alphabetical sequence. The civil action number of the case and the date of the trial should also be placed on each of the exhibit labels. Exhibit lists and copies of exhibits shall be exchanged between parties and the exhibit list filed with the Clerk **at least fourteen (14) days before trial.** The original exhibits and a Judge's copy of the exhibits should be filed with the Clerk at the time of trial. Two copies of the exhibit list are to be filed with the Clerk. It is expected that each party will have a copy of all exhibits to be used at trial.

9.   **JURY INSTRUCTIONS:** Jury instructions shall be prepared and exchanged between the parties and filed with the Clerk (with copies delivered to chambers) **at least seven (7) days before trial.** The Court has prepared stock instructions covering the following State Jury Instruction: X, XX, XXX. Copies of the Court's stock instructions may be obtained from the Court. All instructions shall be prepared in accordance with *civil procedure*. A party objecting to any requested jury instruction shall file at the time of trial, **written objections to jury instructions.**

Notes and Questions 

10.   **TRIAL BRIEFS:** Trial briefs shall be prepared and exchanged between the parties and filed with the Clerk (with copies to chambers) **at least seven (7) days before trial.**

11.   **PROPOSED FINDINGS AND CONCLUSIONS:** If the trial is to the Court, each party shall **at least seven (7) days prior to trial** file with the opposing parties and the Court (with copies to chambers) proposed Findings of Fact and Conclusions of Law supporting their position.

12. **TRIAL DAY:** After the first day of trial, all subsequent trial days will be on an **8:30 a.m. to 1:30 p.m.** schedule.

13. **MODIFICATION:** The Pretrial Order may be modified by stipulation of the parties upon entry of an order by the Court approving such stipulation. Any party may, upon motion and for good cause shown, seek leave of Court modifying the terms of this order, upon such terms and conditions as the Court deems fit. Any party may request a pretrial conference pursuant to *civil procedure* or mediation pursuant to *civil procedure.*

14. **REQUEST TO VACATE TRIAL SETTING:** Any party moving or stipulating to vacate a trial setting shall set forth the reasons for the request and include a representation by counsel that these reasons have been discussed with the client and that the client has no objection to vacating the trial date.

Any vacation or continuance of the trial day shall not change or alter the time frames for the deadlines set forth herein, but the dates for such deadlines will change to the new dates as are established by the date of the new trial setting. Any party may, upon motion and for good cause shown, request different discovery and disclosure dates upon vacation or continuance of the trial

Notes and Questions

date.

15. **SANCTIONS FOR NONCOMPLIANCE:** Failure to timely comply in all respects with the provisions of this order shall subject noncomplying parties to sanctions pursuant to *civil procedure*, which may include:

(A) An order refusing to allow the disobedient party to support or oppose designated claims or defenses, or prohibiting such party from introducing designated matters in evidence;

(B) An order striking out pleadings or parts thereof, or staying further proceedings until the order is obeyed, or dismissing the action or proceeding or any part thereof, or rendering a judgment by default against the disobedient party;

(C) In lieu of any of the foregoing orders or in addition thereto, an order treating as contempt of court the failure to comply;

(D) In lieu of or in addition to any other sanction, the judge shall require the party or the attorney representing such party or both to pay the reasonable expenses incurred because of any noncompliance with this rule, including attorney's fees, unless the judge finds that the noncompliance was substantially justified or that other circumstances make an award of expenses unjust.

IT IS FURTHER ORDERED that no party may rely upon any deadline set forth in this pretrial order as a reason for failing to timely response to discovery or to timely supplement discovery responses pursuant to *civil procedure*.

Notice is hereby given, pursuant to *civil procedure*, that an alternate judge <u>may</u>, be assigned to preside in this case. The following is a list of potential alternate judges: (list of alternate Judges)

Notes and Questions

Unless a party has previously exercised their right to disqualification without cause under civil procedure, each party shall have the right to file one (1) motion for disqualification without cause as to any alternate judge not later than ten (10) days after service of this notice.

DATED this _____ day of _______________, 2005.

BY ORDER OF _______________, District Judge

____
Deputy Clerk/Secretary

<u>CLERK'S CERTIFICATE OF SERVICE</u>

I HEREBY CERTIFY that on the _____ day of _____________, 2007, I caused to be served a true and correct copy of the foregoing by the method indicated below, and addressed to the following:

(Attorney for Plaintiff)
☐ U.S. MAIL
☐ TELECOPY (FAX) to: //

(Attorney for Defendant)
☐ U.S. Mail
☐ TELECOPY (FAX) to: //

CLERK OF THE DISTRICT COURT

By: _________________________________
DEPUTY

FIGURE 3.1 Sample of a Pre-Trial Scheduling Order with Exhibit list form to follow

Notes and Questions

LIST OF EXHIBITS

CASE NUMBER: ______________________
DATE OF TRIAL: ______________________
TITLE OF CASE: ______________________

☐ PLAINTIFF'S EXHIBITS (list numerically)
☐ DEFENDANT'S EXHIBITS (list alphabetically)
☐ THIRD PARTY EXHIBITS   STATE PARTY ______________________

No.	Description	By Stip	Offered	Received	Refused	Reserve

FIGURE 3.1 Sample of a Pre-Trial Scheduling Order with Exhibit list form

As you can see in **Figure 3.1**, the deadlines include, but are not limited to, discovery, witness identification, expert witness disclosure, as well as exhibit identification and production. You and your attorney must finalize <u>all</u> discovery prior to the discovery deadline date. All witnesses and proposed trial exhibits must be identified by the date indicated in the scheduling order. If you have an expert, you must identify your expert witness by the date specified in the schedule.

TIP: When listing your witnesses you wish to testify at trial, keep your list short and sweet. Just have the people who you believe are seriously going to make a difference. It costs money to have each witness served with a subpoena, it costs money to interview them, it costs money to have them questioned at trial, and it costs money to have them cross examined at trial. If they don't have enough information to really help your case, consider not having them appear. Think this list through thoroughly.

Trial preparation, such as discovery, exhibits, witnesses, interviewing witnesses, subpoenaing witnesses, takes a lot of time for your attorney to accomplish and in turn costs you a lot of money. After the discovery phase you should be able to review all of the information in your case and decide if this is still a battle worth fighting. Your attorney should evaluate your matter and give you the up-side, the down-side, your best case scenario, your worst case scenario, and what the <u>likely</u> outcome should be, based on his knowledge, experience, expertise, and

Notes and Questions

information received during the advancement of your case.

You should be pretty familiar with the process regarding documents, discovery, exhibits, and getting your matter ready for trial. Another thing you must be aware of is regarding expert witnesses. If you have an expert witness, you can have your expert appear at trial to testify live or have your attorney take the expert's deposition in lieu of live trial testimony. Your attorney can best advise you whether or not the live testimony is necessary, however, you should be aware of the option to depose in lieu of live testimony. It can be quite a bit less expensive than having the expert appear at trial.

I have heard of an expert witness physician charging $8,000 for one day of live trial testimony!

You should discuss experts in detail with your attorney because they can run your costs up considerably. Experts usually require a deposit and lots of advance notice if not needed. Be aware of what the expert's requirements are before you engage them. Your attorney should advise you thoroughly on experts.

Everything you have is now prepared and ready to proceed to trial. Your evidence, exhibits, witnesses, experts, transcripts are all ordered, copied and provided to the opposing side within the month prior to your scheduled trial date. Trial itself is not nearly as glamorous as it is made to look on television. In fact, it is nothing like that at all. There isn't any Boston Legal type shenanigans, no surprise witnesses, and The Practice sure makes everyone seem beautiful huh? The reality is trial is with regular people who live in your community and there are very specific rules which must be followed. Many cases settle on the courthouse steps because of the expense of trial and the attorneys' perception of the possible outcome. Keep this in mind; It is never too late to settle. Trial is stressful and exhausting. Even your best case scenario is costly, your worst case, is extremely expensive.

At the beginning of trial, the attorneys submit the exhibits to the court, the opposing party's attorney may object to the exhibit, and the judge may or may not enter the exhibit. If opposing party's attorney does not object, the exhibit is entered into by Stipulation, or agreed to between the parties. The judge's clerk will mark each exhibit entered as Trial Exhibit #1, #2, #3, and so on. Those exhibits are the only exhibits the jury will be allowed to view. There are rules of evidence

Notes and Questions 

which dictate the procedure regarding exhibits. You can have the best evidence but not have gone through the procedure correctly only to have it denied admission and the jury will never even see it. Many good cases have been lost due to misunderstanding the rules of evidence and proper civil procedure. It is essential you have an attorney who is familiar with evidentiary rules and a master of civil procedure.

Every trial is different depending on your judge, state, case and style of the attorneys involved. There are standards of practice and you should discuss exactly what to expect with your attorney prior to the day of your trial. Do not wait until the night before trial to do this. You should meet with your attorney at least a week prior to trial to discuss these matters. This should give you enough time to digest the information and be ready on your trial date. When you discuss what to expect at trial, be sure to write it down. Trial is tense, emotional, overwhelming and scary all at once and it is easy to get flustered and confused. If you have notes to rely upon you can stay better focused.

After trial, there may be post-trial issues such as cost and attorney fee disputes, motions for reconsideration, motions for contempt, appeal, and more. Your attorney can advise you as to whether or not he feels any post-trial briefing is required or if an appeal is appropriate.

You now have a basic idea of what to expect during each phase of your lawsuit. Let's review one last time; You filed a complaint, or answered one, possibly mediated some issues, entered the Twilight Zone of the Discovery Phase. You asked and answered Interrogatories, asked for and produced documents, and probably had your deposition taken. Once you received your trial date, you and your attorney discussed experts, witnesses, and exhibits and complied with the Pre-Trial Scheduling Order. You also experienced trial and perhaps some post trial briefings.

Fun huh? I didn't think so. I'm sure you have lost a night or two of sleep during the whole process.

If you haven't gone through this process yet, now you have some idea what to expect and can be somewhat prepared. I caution you, however, even when you know what to expect, when you are involved in it, it is an entirely different experience and the stress is immeasurable.

Notes and Questions

I once heard that going through a divorce lawsuit is as difficult and stressful as experiencing the death of a loved one. I believe it.

During the Pre-Trial preparation and trial you have many opportunities to save some money. Here are some of those ways……

Other Things and Ways to Save, Phase 3

- Time is Money! By the time you get to the trial preparations you are well aware of this fact and have hopefully mastered some of the time saving techniques offered in this book.

- Discuss settlement options with your attorney. Trial is expensive; it may be worth it to settle the matter.

- Organization is crucial. Theoretically, from the very filing of the Complaint you are in "trial preparation." Most of the work is already done; However, the month before trial is when the information gathered in the discovery phase is organized to support your issues.

- Read your Pre-Trial Scheduling Order and calendar those dates so you know what is coming and when it is due. If you can settle the matter prior to the attorney's staff having created all of the exhibits and interviewed the witnesses, you will have saved. If you wait too long, you will have already incurred the expense for trial preparation, regardless of whether or not you go to trial.

- If you are very organized, ask your attorney if you can assist by making your exhibit copies yourself. Depending on the cost of in-house copying, you may be able to save a bundle. Beware, however, if you are not organized, you will pay more for the paralegal to sort your disheveled copies.

- If you believe you are close to settlement, try to settle prior to the exhibit preparation. You can possibly save thousands of dollars in time and copy charges, depending on the size of your case.

- When you are approaching trial, you and your attorney should now decide if any of the depositions yielded enough information to warrant the cost of ordering the transcripts. If not, don't order them. If so, order them early enough that you don't incur any rush charges.

- It is very expensive to have expert witnesses testify at trial. Their fees can be astronomical. If an expert is needed, discuss the possibility of taking the Deposition in Lieu of Live Trial Testimony. It is usually a fraction of the cost associated with having the expert appear live at trial. You should discuss with your attorney whether or not the presence of the expert at trial is necessary.

Notes and Questions 

(\$) Be prepared for trial, know your issues, know what your case is worth to you and discuss all possible outcomes with your attorney. Know what your bottom line is to settle. Discuss with your attorney your best and worst case scenarios.

(\$) Discuss the proposed length of the trial with your attorney. Is it really necessary to schedule a three day trial or can it be done in two?

(\$) Are you proceeding on an emotional decision or a legal one? Do you intend to proceed on principle or ego rather than facts? Sometimes it is bad business to proceed, and good business to end it. Be secure about your decision to proceed to trial.

Lawsuits can be handled in all kinds of different ways. It is not as black and white as a lot of people think. Your lawyer will advise you on what he or she believes is best for you with respect to your particular case. You should now have the general idea of how it works and what to expect. This is the story of You and Your Lawsuit.

Things I need to discuss with my attorney regarding mediation, settlement, arbitration or even dismissal of my lawsuit.

Finally........

Just a few other things to think about.

There are other things that happen during the lawsuit that don't necessarily fit into any one of the "phases" and you need to be aware of them in case any pop up during your matter.

Some things you may experience are Mediation, Arbitration or Case Dismissal. There are several books written on the subject of Mediation and when you are involved in mediation I suggest you read one, or some, of those books. Arbitration and Case Dismissal should be discussed with your attorney specifically.

Additionally, throughout the entire process of your suit, you should keep records and notes of all events. For example, if you make a phone call to your attorney's office, attend a hearing, attend a deposition, any event which takes place related to your lawsuit; you should take copious notes of what was discussed, what took place, a summary of the event. Use these notes later on when reviewing your bills and when reviewing your matter for you own deposition or trial appearance. In **Appendix A** herein, you will find forms for you to copy and use throughout your suit. Each serves its purpose. Specifically you will find a Telephone Log, Appointment Log, and Hearing Log. Each time you speak to, meet with or go to a hearing with your attorney, you should record the event and what took place. When you get your bill, cross reference your notes with your bill. Not only will this help you to stay informed and in touch with your case, you will be able to verify each entry on your bill. It's almost like balancing your checkbook register. When the statement comes in, you check it off in your register. So, when your bill comes in, you check off each entry with your notes and logs. It's as simple as that!

Notes and Questions 

And Finally, Other Things and Ways to Save

($) Mediation is a good way to settle a matter and save further costs and fees.

($) Arbitration can be a less expensive alternative to Trial.

($) At any time during the process, you can settle your matter.

($) Keep notes of every event on the enclosed log sheets. Cross reference those notes with your bills to ensure accuracy.

($) Use your notes to prepare for depositions and hearings. Being informed saves you money.

Notes and Questions

More questions I have which have not been answered here.

All Too Frequently Asked Questions

Some things you just hear over and over again…..

Is this attorney any good?

Well, I've heard this a lot, however, what kind of employee would say no?   Of course the employee is going to say the attorney is good, so it's a useless question. If you are unsure, call the American Bar Association, the Better Business Bureau or another attorney's office in town and ask about the attorney. You can usually get a good feel by the responses you get from the staff of another office.

How much is this going to cost?

There is usually no way of telling exactly how much your case is going to cost. Only when you get a Flat Fee will you know. Otherwise, the variables which will effect your costs include; the type of your case; how much you are willing to spend; how complex the issues are; how much of a fight the other side is capable of putting up; what the attorney on the other side is like; what your attorney is like; if the attorneys have a good working relationship; if you go to trial or settle at mediation….and more. The list of variables is endless.

How long will this take?

There are so many variables that it is virtually impossible to tell exactly how long your matter will take. There are general benchmarks depending on the kind of case, but even then you cannot tell precisely how long it's going to take.

What happens at a status conference?

A status conference is about getting the parties and their attorneys together with the judge to let the judge know the "status" of the case and where each party is in the discovery phase. Shortly after a status conference your matter will usually get set for trial. The date for the trial will depend on the judge's calendar and at what point you are in your case. The judge will set the trial date out a long time, possibly even several months, to get the parties moving, but still leave enough time to get the discovery process finished prior to the set trial date.

What happens at a pretrial conference?

Pretrial conferences are scheduled to let the judge know if you are close to settling or all set to proceed to trial. It is usually a short conference with the attorneys and the judge, although some judges do require the parties to attend. In some states the pretrial conference can be done by telephone.

Why doesn't the attorney ever call me back?

Most attorneys are very busy with several different cases and there are times when they just can't call you back. When they are engrossed in **your** case, you will be glad the attorney keeps focused on your matter. It all evens out in the end. If you cannot get a call back, your best bet, initially, is to try to get information passed through the paralegal or secretary.

Why won't he take my calls, I always get put through to you?

There are several issues within the scope and abilities of the paralegal or secretary. Also, keep in mind, the attorney might be preparing for another matter and cannot be interrupted. There are many variables and most likely the attorney wants to attend to you, however, cannot do it personally at that moment and therefore forwards your call to the paralegal or secretary. If the issue requires the attorney's immediate attention, the paralegal or secretary will forward that information and your attorney will evaluate the situation and act accordingly.

Why did you do that?

Because it needed to be done in order to prosecute or defend your matter.

What is Discovery?

Discovery is the process in which information is gathered to prove your claims and/or disprove the opposing side's claims. (See Glossary and Phase 2 regarding Discovery tools.)

What are Interrogatories? Can they ask that?

Interrogatories are written questions that must be responded to in writing, under oath, within a prescribed amount of time. Yes, they can ask that. (See Glossary and Phase 2 regarding Discovery tools.)

Why do they need those documents? Do I have to give them to them? Can they ask for those?

Yes, unless your attorney advises otherwise and requests a protection order, you do have to produce them. My rule of thumb is to always produce the requested documents to your

attorney's office and your attorney will produce them if they do not fall under any privileged documents rule. If they are privileged documents, your attorney will request a protection of those documents. Should (s)he not receive the protection order, then the documents are already with your attorney and (s)he can produce them quickly. The other side requests documents they think may lead to admissible evidence, theoretically. If you are concerned about the documents requested, discuss this with your attorney right away. (See Glossary and Phase 2 regarding Discovery tools).

Can the other side just set my Deposition anytime they want?
Yes. Most offices will cooperate with each other to schedule a Deposition, but if they don't get a response soon enough or if they are non-cooperative, they can set your Deposition whenever it is convenient for them, not you.

What are objections?
Some attorneys ask things that are not within the scope of your state's rules of civil procedure. When this happens an objection is made, either orally at a hearing or by brief. For example, sometimes in the Interrogatories there is a question asked that is not "allowed." Your attorney will file an Objection to that specific question in his Response to Interrogatories.

How does a jury get picked?
The court goes to Voter Registry, sends out a Jury Duty letter, then the attorneys pick from the pool assigned to their case.

What is voir dire?
An examination by the attorneys of prospective jurors, under oath, to determine whether or not they are suitable to become jurors. Or, in other words, picking members of the jury.

Is a character witness necessary?
Not always. Your attorney can advise you whether it is necessary in your specific case.

Can my child speak with the judge?
Not normally. Most judges frown upon putting children on the stand. Most of the issues are between the adults and Judges like to keep the children out of it and out of the courtroom.

Why do they need my bank statements?
Several reasons. For example, if you are dividing assets, say in a divorce or dissolution of a business, the bank statements can tell a lot about how much money there is and where the money is spent or held. If, in your case, your attorney feels it is privileged information (s)he will act accordingly.

If we are both on the bank account...why do I have to get copies?
If you are the primary person on the account or are receiving the statements directly, then you would normally need to provide copies of the statements.

Why does the dentist keep billing me when my ex owes his portion?

> Because as parents you are both legally responsible, however, it isn't the care provider's responsibility to get the proper amount due by each parent. The parents should figure it out between themselves. And if you sign as responsible party on the form, the dentist sees you as the liable party.

I sent a letter to the judge, how come he has not responded?

> You are not supposed to communicate directly with the judge unless you are representing yourself and have provided the opposing side a copy of the communication. All communication with the judge or court must be sent to the other side as well.

I have been contacted by my soon-to-be ex's attorney. Is that ok?

> Not normally. Once you have hired an attorney, you should not discuss your matter with the opposing counsel. You should inform opposing to contact your attorney directly. You should also inform your attorney that the other attorney has contacted you directly.

I have been contacted by my soon-to- be ex. Can I talk to him/her?

> Yes. The parties may speak to each other unless they have a Protection Order barring any contact. The parties may communicate and even settle their matter. As long as there isn't a Protection Order and the communication is productive and not harassing, it should be permitted.

Do you have to go to school to become a paralegal?

> No. You don't have to, although more and more firms are requiring their paralegals to have either a four-year degree, a certificate from an American Bar Association approved program or several years of legal experience.

Can I help do any of the work to lower my bill?

> The answer to this will depend on you, your case and the attorney you hire. There are always things you can do to help save money. If you are organized, provide the information requested quickly and neatly, call with questions written out and call only when you **need** to call, you can save an arm and a leg.

Notes and Questions 

Terms I don't understand and need to discuss with my attorney

Glossary

More and More and More Terms You Should know.

One of the first things you should do is purchase a Law Dictionary. As soon as you get a legal document, look up any term which you find confusing or you are unsure about. I have included some of the most common terms used and some which I have used here in this book for your convenience. I have tried to make these terms easy to understand. If you still don't understand a term, ask your attorney to clarify those terms for you or look them up in your new dictionary.

Admissions	Discovery tool. Pleading: One party sends a Request for Admission to the other party. The receiving party has a specific number of days to respond to the request or the request is deemed "admitted." In civil procedure a request for admission is a pretrial discovery device by which one party asks another for a positive affirmation or denial of a material fact or allegation at issue.
Affidavit	A written statement made under oath before an officer of the court or a notary public or other person who has been duly authorized so to act.
Amend(ment)	To alter or to improve upon. An Amended pleading is to change by making an addition to or subtraction from an already existing pleading.
Associate	Attorney working at the firm who is not a partner.
Billing increment	The minimum amount of time the attorney bills. For example, most attorneys bill in 6 minute increments, but some bill in 15 minute increments.
Brief	A written argument concentrating on legal points and authorities which is used by the lawyer to convey to the court the essential facts of his client's case.
Child Support	The amount of money a person must pay to help support their children after a divorce or custody proceeding.
Civil Procedure	Rules and procedures to be adhered to in the process of advancing your case through the system.
Claim	The assertion of right to money or property.
Complaint	In a civil action the first pleading of the Plaintiff setting out the facts on which the claim for relief is based.
Counsel	Your attorney or lawyer.
Court clerk	A person who enters the documents into the court docket.

Notes and Questions

Terms I don't understand and need to discuss with my attorney

Court reporter	A person hired by either party, or the court, specially trained on a specialized machine (transcriber) to type the transcript of every word spoken during the procedure, whether it's a deposition, hearing, or trial.
Court Rules	Specific rules to the court within which your suit has been filed. Some states local rules are different in each county. When prosecuting a case you must produce documents in full compliance per the local court rules within which your suit is filed.
Cross Claim	A claim by the defendant of a suit against another party.
Deposition	A question and answer session which is recorded by a court reporter and a transcript produced.
Discovery	Information gathering phase of a lawsuit, including but not limited to Interrogatories, Request for Production of Documents, Request for Admissions, and Depositions.
E-transcripts	Electronic Transcript of a hearing or deposition. Can be emailed or sent to you on a disk.
Hearing	Meeting at the courthouse with the Judge to discuss and receive a ruling on issues raised and set to be heard.
Interrogatories	Written questions from one party to another.
Notice of Service	Document filed with the court indicating that specific documents listed were served on the other party and how said service was made, either personally, by fax, by mail, etc.
Paralegal	Professional working under the supervision of an attorney. A paralegal cannot give legal advice, sign documents or appear for you in court.
Pleading	Document written in a specific format and filed with the court.
Prayer	Demand or request for specifics used at the end of a Complaint, Cross-Complaint, Counter-Complaint or Answer.
Procedure	The procedure which dictates how each thing is to be done. This is defined by the County, State, or Federal Rules.
Production of documents	Requests from one party to another to produce documents and things as part of the discovery tools listed herein.
Service of Process	When a person hands documents to another and says, "You have been served". This process server then files an Affidavit of Service with the court.
Statute of Limitations	Any law which fixes the time within which parties must take judicial action to enforce rights or else be thereafter barred from enforcing them.
Stipulation	A signed agreement between the parties.
Subpoena	Order from the Court for a person to appear at a specific time and place.
Transcripts	Written transcript of the spoken words at a hearing or deposition.

Notes and Questions

Websites I should go to and web searches I can do to get more informed.

Websites and Links

Links to websites and places to help you learn more about what to expect during your lawsuit.

State Websites:

http://www.hg.org/usstates

This website lists every state in the US. Once you are at the homepage, on the left border go down to States' Law, click on States' Law and you will get every state in the nation. Once you click on the state you are interested in, you can access the state home page, as well as tons of information on that state. This is a website worth checking out.

Web searches to try:

For Example, go to a search engine, such as Google.com, and type the following phrases and see what comes up....

- Child Support Calculations (name your state)
- Divorce Forms (name your state)
- Statutes (name your state)
- (Your state) Bar Association
- American Bar Association

Other Links:

www.MidnightShadow.net
www.GirleeGirlUSA.com

Notes and Questions 

I need to order this book for a friend who needs to have this guide!

Order Form:

To order another copy of this workbook, get on our mailing list and receive notification of other publications by this author, please forward your information below. You can also download an E-book from www.MidnightShadow.net and get the book today.

Name: ____

Address: ____

City: ___________________________ State: ___________ Zip: ________________

Email: ____

☐ Please send me _______ copies of **You and Your Lawsuit: An Insider's Guide to Saving Money**. I have included my check or money order payable to Midnight Shadow Publishing in the amount of $29.95 plus $4.00 for shipping and handling for each copy ordered.

☐ Please include my name and email address for email notifications regarding publications from this author and upcoming book signing events.

**We will never sell your email address and we use it only to
notify you of upcoming publications and events.**

We will never give out any email address for any purpose to any other company or individual.

<u>www.MidnightShadow.net</u>

Appendix A:

Forms to help you stay organized along the way.

See the following attached forms:

Phone Log

Appointment Log

Hearing Log

Notes and Questions Forms

PHONE LOG

Date: _______________________________

Spoke with: ____

Call Start Time:________ Call End Time:________ Total Minutes:______

Call Notes:

____

____

____

____

____

____

____

____

PHONE LOG

Date: _______________________________

Spoke with: ____

Call Start Time:________ Call End Time:________ Total Minutes:_______

Call Notes:

____

____

____

____

____

____

____

APPOINTMENT LOG

Date: _______________________________

Spoke with: ____

Start Time:_____________ End Time:_____________ Total Minutes:_______

Notes:

____

____

____

____

____

____

APPOINTMENT LOG

Date: _______________________________

Spoke with: ____

Start Time:____________ End Time:____________ Total Minutes:______

Notes:

____

____

____

____

____

____

____

HEARING LOG

Date: _______________________________

Judge: ____

Reason for Hearing: ____
(Motion for Discovery, Motion to Compel, Status Conference, etc.)

Start Time:____________ End Time:____________ Total Minutes:______

Notes:

____

____

____

____

____

____

____

____

____

HEARING LOG

Date: _______________________________

Judge: ____

Reason for Hearing: ____
(Motion for Discovery, Motion to Compel, Status Conference, etc.)

Start Time:_____________ End Time:_____________ Total Minutes:_______

Notes:

____

____

____

____

____

____

____

____

____

Notes and Questions

Things I need to discuss with my attorney during this phase of the lawsuit.

Notes and Questions

Things I need to discuss with my attorney during this phase of the lawsuit.

Notes and Questions

Notes and Questions

Notes and Questions 

Notes and Questions

www.ingramcontent.com/pod-product-compliance
Lightning Source LLC
Chambersburg PA
CBHW080301030726
47593CB00009B/2581